You Can Write a Story!

A Story-Writing Recipe for Kids

by Lisa Bullard

illustrated by Deborah Haley Melmon

TWO CAN

Minnetonka, Minnesota

For the best ingredients in my life's favorite stories: Matthew, Alex, Sam, Caitlin, and Laura

—L. B.

To Ernie and Gracie—
my very own crunchy characters

—D. H. M.

Two-Can Publishing
11571 K-Tel Drive
Minnetonka, MN 55343
www.two-canpublishing.com

Text copyright © 2007 by Lisa Bullard
Illustrations copyright © 2007 by Deborah Haley Melmon
Edited by Jill Anderson
Designed by Lois A. Rainwater

Library of Congress Cataloging-in-Publication Data

Bullard, Lisa.
You can write a story! : a story-writing recipe for kids / by Lisa Bullard ; illustrated by Deborah Haley Melmon.
p. cm.
Summary: "Explains the ingredients and steps involved in writing a fictional story, from start to finish. Includes brainstorming activities and ideas for sharing the story with others"—Provided by publisher.
Includes bibliographical references and index.
ISBN-13: 978-1-58728-587-5 (hardcover w/wire-o binding)
1. English language—Composition and exercises—Study and teaching (Elementary)—Juvenile literature.
2. Creative writing (Elementary education)—Juvenile literature. 3. Language arts (Elementary)—Juvenile literature.
I. Melmon, Deborah, ill. II. Title.

LB1576.B887 2007

372.62'3—dc22   2006016771

Printed in Malaysia

1 2 3 4 5 11 10 09 08 07

Table of Contents

MARK TWAIN

INTRODUCTION:	A Story-Writing Recipe	4
CHAPTER 1:	Basic Ingredients	6
CHAPTER 2:	Special Flavorings	8
CHAPTER 3:	Crunchy Characters	10
CHAPTER 4:	Spicy Settings	14
CHAPTER 5:	Stir Things Up	18
CHAPTER 6:	Let's Start Cooking	22
CHAPTER 7:	Turn Up the Heat	26
CHAPTER 8:	Out of the Oven	30
CHAPTER 9:	Tempting Titles	32
CHAPTER 10:	Taste Test	34
CHAPTER 11:	Borrow Some Sugar	36
CHAPTER 12:	Share the Feast	38
CHAPTER 13:	Are You Still Hungry?	40
SILLY, CHILLY BEAR	A story by Lisa Bullard	41
GLOSSARY		46
FOR FURTHER READING		47
INDEX		47

Introduction
A Story-Writing Recipe

You can write a story! This book will help you learn how. It is a little bit like making cookies. The difference is, we're going to cook up a story!

When you make cookies, you use a **recipe**. The recipe gives you directions for making the cookies. You can use a recipe to write a story, too. The recipe will take you step-by-step. Before you know it, you will have a finished story!

Even with the help of a recipe, cooks have to practice their cooking skills. Writers need to practice their writing skills, too. This book will help you practice. The more you practice, the better your stories will be.

Cooking up stories can be more fun than making cookies! So let's get started.

Grammy's Cookie Recipe
1. Mix together butter, eggs, sugar and extract.
2. Add dry ingredients and stir.
3. Bake 10 minutes in 350° oven. Frost when cool.

FLOUR

SUG

LEMON EXTRACT

One important writing skill is called **brainstorming**. Brainstorming means working your mind to think of lots of new ideas. Writers often brainstorm before they begin a story. They might brainstorm again in the middle of their story. We will practice brainstorming many different times as we follow the special story-writing recipe.

HERE'S A TIP

Make sure you have lots of paper and a sharp pencil. But don't worry about erasing when you brainstorm. That just wastes time. List all your ideas, good or bad. Sound out the words you can't spell. Draw a picture if you can't think of the right word. It might get messy, just like when you cook. But that just means your brain is working hard!

Chapter 1 Basic Ingredients

The first thing a recipe gives you is a list of **ingredients.** Ingredients are the different things that you mix together. Cookies have ingredients like flour, sugar, and eggs. Your stories will have many ingredients too. But you can't buy these ingredients at the grocery store. They will come from your own imagination!

We are going to start with story ingredients that you really like. Take out a piece of paper and a pencil. Answer these questions:

1. What is your favorite animal?

2. If you could travel anywhere, where would you visit? *Hint: You can even choose the bottom of the ocean or the planet Mars or a made-up land.*

3. What is an activity that you really enjoy? *Hint: It is good to choose an activity that is very creative or active. Think of sports, music, art, or games you play with other people.*

The ingredients in a story all have special names. Look at the animal that you picked. That animal will become a story ingredient called a **character.** Characters can also be people. Characters can even be aliens or ghosts or monsters! A story can have many different characters. The most important one is called the main character. That's who your story will be about.

You also wrote down a place you would like to visit. That will become part of a story ingredient called a **setting.** The setting is both the place and time of your story. That means where and when the story happens. You already chose a place. Now ask yourself, Will your story be set at a different time in history? Will it be set in the future? Or is it happening now?

The third thing you wrote down is an activity. This activity will help you build action into your story. Action pushes a story forward. Your readers will like your story if you add a lot of action.

See how many ingredients you already have? You're already on your way to writing a story!

Chapter 2 Special Flavorings

When you make cookies, you add **flavorings** to the basic ingredients. Flavorings are what make different kinds of cookies taste the way they do. They make chocolate cookies taste different than peanut butter cookies.

The stories we are writing are called **fiction.** That means we are making them up. They didn't really happen. But there are many kinds of fiction. Each one has its own flavor.

Some fiction is **realistic.** A realistic story includes many facts. Do you like learning new information? Then maybe you would like to write a realistic story. Here is an example: The animal I picked for my character is a polar bear. For a realistic story, I would have my polar bear eat seals.

Or would you rather write a **fantasy?** A fantasy includes things that don't happen in the real world. In a fantasy, my polar bear might eat only pineapples and pizza. Or maybe my polar bear would talk like a person! Do you like to use your imagination? Then maybe you would like to write a fantasy.

You can also write a story that mixes fact and fantasy. Or maybe you want to write a funny story with jokes. Or a scary story about monsters. Or a mystery. You get to decide the flavor of your story. That is your job as the writer!

HERE'S A TIP

Write the kind of story that you would most like to read.

Chapter 3
Crunchy Characters

Do you remember what the ingredient called a character is? Characters are creatures or people. They are also the stars of your story. It is good to make your characters interesting. I call that making characters "crunchy." That way there is a lot for readers to chew on!

Creating characters is kind of like meeting new people. It is good to learn a lot about them. You may decide to have many characters in your story. But for now, let's focus on your main character. To get to know that character, you are going to conduct an **interview.** Maybe you have seen someone being interviewed on TV. An interview is when you ask somebody a whole bunch of questions. You learn about them through their answers.

Brainstorming Activity

Interview Your Main Character

STEP 1: Your first step is to think up a lot of interview questions. Pretend you are meeting somebody for the first time. What questions would you ask them? What questions would help you get to know them better? When you brainstorm, you want to think of lots of ideas. So write down lots of questions.

Your job right now is just to think of questions. Don't start answering them yet! Here are a few questions to get you started:

- ★ What is your name?
- ★ How old are you?
- ★ Where do you sleep?
- ★ What is your favorite food?
- ★ Do you have a family?
- ★ What do you look like?

Now keep going! Write down more interview questions.

STEP 2: Now that you have a list of interview questions, it's time to work on the answers. But you are not going to answer the questions for yourself. Instead, you are going to make up the answers your main character would give!

Remember that your character is an animal. Look at your list of questions. Answer each question the way your main character would answer. Remember to include facts if you are writing a realistic story. Really work your imagination if you are writing a fantasy. See how many things you can learn about your main character!

Additional Ingredients for Your Crunchy Characters

There is a name for all the things you learned about your character. They are called **descriptive details.** They are another important story ingredient. Descriptive details give your reader extra information. They make your story come alive. They create pictures in the reader's head. For example, my polar bear story might say: *Pete is the world's only purple polar bear. He gets so cold he shivers all the time.* Now you have a picture in your head of Pete. The details helped make that picture.

PRACTICE WITH ME
Interview a Character

Do you need help with interviewing? Let's practice together. We will interview my main character.

QUESTION: What is your name?
ANSWER FOR MY CHARACTER: Pete the polar bear

QUESTION: What is your favorite food?
ANSWER: Pineapples!

QUESTION: What do you look like?
ANSWER: I look like a regular polar bear except I am purple.

QUESTION: Who is your best friend?
ANSWER: Nick the narwhal.

Can you tell from my answers that I decided to write a funny fantasy?

Ship To: Pete the Polar Bear The Arctic

HERE'S A TIP

Think of your character as your new friend. What would you want to know about them?

Chapter 4
Spicy Settings

Descriptive details will make your character more interesting. Good stories also include details about your setting. Remember, your setting is the place and time of your story. Look at your answer to question 2 on page 6. What place did you pick for your setting?

You want to make your readers feel like they are inside that setting. Can they smell something spicy? Or hear scary sounds? Descriptive details can make the setting seem real. But how do you do this in your story?

Brainstorming Activity

Create Setting Details

STEP 1: Get very comfortable. You might even want to lie down. But keep your pencil and paper handy. Now, forget about the room around you. Instead, move inside your imagination. Pretend you are moving around in your setting. Pay careful attention to everything that is there. Sometimes it helps to close your eyes for a few minutes.

STEP 2: When you have a detailed picture in your mind, take out your pencil and paper so you can make some notes. What does your story setting look like? What colors can you see? Is your setting a jungle with lots of trees? Are you surrounded by snow and ice, or swimming over beautiful coral reefs? What do you see inside your setting? Write it down.

STEP 3: Cup your hand around your ear. What does your story setting sound like? Listen very hard inside your setting. Are the noises loud or soft? Are there car horns and sirens, like in a big city? Or are there birds singing in a deep forest? What do you hear inside your setting? Write it down.

chirp

STEP 4: Reach out your hand. Pretend that you are touching things in your setting. What do they feel like? Are the things smooth or rough? Are they slimy or dry? Now think about the air inside your story setting. Is it hot and wet, like a jungle? Or is it very cold, like the planet Mars? What can you touch and feel inside your setting? Write it down.

STEP 5: Take a big sniff. Bigger! Pretend that you are smelling things inside your setting. Do you smell pine trees or flowers? Or do you smell stinky rotten eggs? Do you smell popcorn from a movie theater? Or fish from the salty ocean? What do you smell inside your setting? Write it down.

STEP 6: Chomp your teeth together. Pretend that your character has invited you to dinner. You are eating their favorite food. If you are lucky, you may get to eat pizza or chocolate cake. But if you have a realistic lion for your character, you will be eating raw meat for dinner! What things can you taste inside your setting? Write them down.

Additional Ingredients for Your Spicy Settings

Take a look at all the details about your setting. Do you know what tools we used to find them? They are called the **five senses.** That is the name for seeing, hearing, touching, smelling, and tasting. Remember to use these tools when you write!

People often pay the most attention to the things they see. So surprise your readers with sounds, smells, tastes, or touches. You do not have to use all five senses in every story. But try to include different kinds of details. If your character is a dog, you will probably want to include lots of smells!

HERE'S A TIP

Use all five senses when you write.

PRACTICE WITH ME
Setting Details

Are you having trouble understanding how to use your five senses? Then let's practice together. The place that I picked for my setting is Hawaii. Here are some descriptive details I can think of. What else can you add to my list?

WHAT CAN I SEE IN HAWAII?

blue ocean water, swimsuits in all colors, surfers

WHAT CAN I HEAR IN HAWAII?

the sound of waves, special island music, birds

WHAT CAN I FEEL IN HAWAII?

warm sand, gentle wind, hot sun

WHAT CAN I SMELL IN HAWAII?

suntan lotion, flowers, sea salt

WHAT CAN I TASTE IN HAWAII?

pineapples, fish, coconuts

Chapter 5 Stir Things Up

Many recipes include a step where you stir ingredients together. When you stir things up in a story, you create **conflict.** Conflict is all the problems in a story. Problems are a very important ingredient! They make your reader want to keep reading. The reader wants to find out how the problems are solved. Problems can make stories funny or scary. Problems pack a story full of adventure.

Brainstorming Activity

Stirring Up Story Problems

STEP 1: Who is your animal character? Where is your setting? What activity did you write down for question 3 on page 6?

STEP 2: Mix these basic ingredients together. What do you get? When I mix my basic ingredients together, I get a polar bear who wants to water-ski in Hawaii. Does your mix seem as strange as mine? Don't worry! A strange mix is a good thing. It will help you think of story problems. It helps create the new ingredient called conflict.

STEP 3: Now it is time to brainstorm a list of story problems. Look at the mix you made with your character, setting, and activity. What problems can you see? Write down everything that comes into your head. Maybe there are also other kinds of problems to add. Your character could have problems at home or at school. Or with friends or family. Keep going! You might not use all of these problems. But lots of good ideas will make writing your story easier.

PRACTICE
WITH ME
Story Problems

Do you need some help thinking of problems? Let's practice together. We'll work on problem ideas for my story. Remember what I get when I mix my ingredients together? I get a polar bear who wants to water-ski in Hawaii. There are sure a lot of problems with that!

HERE ARE SOME PROBLEMS FOR MY BRAINSTORMING LIST:

★ How would a polar bear get to Hawaii?

★ What if the polar bear gets lost on the way to Hawaii?

★ Hawaii is too warm for polar bears.

★ They don't make water skis for polar bears.

★ Polar bears don't know how to water-ski.

★ A real polar bear might try to eat the boat driver!

★ What if my polar bear feels lonely because he doesn't have many friends?

★ What if my polar bear has an enemy?

★ What if my polar bear gets laughed at because he is purple?

★ What if my polar bear can't handle being cold?

Can you think of other problems for my polar bear? What would make my story funny? What would make my story scary? What would add adventure?

Now think of more problems for your story! Don't be afraid to be creative!

HERE'S A TIP

Problems are a good thing in stories! Stories with lots of problems are much more interesting.

Extra Food for Thought

Does your brain have room to think about another ingredient? This ingredient is connected to the problems in your story. It is your characters' **emotions.**

Emotions are how a character is feeling. A character who has a big problem might feel angry at first. The character might show this anger by stomping around. Another problem might make your character feel sad. The character might show this by crying.

When the problem is fixed, your character's emotions will change. Then your character might feel happy or proud.

What emotions do you think your character will feel in your story? Make a list of ideas.

Chapter 6
Let's Start Cooking

You have a big mix of ingredients. You have a character, a setting, action, details, and conflict. It's time to start writing your story! But the beginning is the hardest part for some writers.

Sometimes people are afraid to start. They think they will write it the wrong way. Don't let that stop you! This is your **rough draft**. Another name for that is a sloppy copy. You will have a chance to go back and fix things later. We will talk about that in chapter 10. For now, just write what comes into your head.

Remember not to worry too much about spelling or other mistakes. Do your best with the rules of writing, but don't let the rules get you stuck.

You might want to skip lines, or double-space. That means write a line of your story, and then leave a line blank. Then write another line. That way, you will have room to add or fix things later.

Remember all the time you spent brainstorming? You have already written down a lot of ideas. It should not be too hard to keep writing. So, let's get this story cooking!

Brainstorming Activity

Write a Beginning

STEP 1: Look at the answers your character gave in the interview. What does the reader need to know right away? Mark two or three details on your interview list.

STEP 2: Look at your story problem list. What problem could start off your story? Mark one or two good ideas on your problem list.

STEP 3: Look at your setting details. What are the most important things for the reader to know? Mark those details.

STEP 4: Look at the things that you have marked on your lists. How can you mix them together to grab the reader's attention? Brainstorm many different beginnings. Keep going until you have one you really like. Write that beginning on a new piece of paper. Your story is off to a great start!

I like this one ↓

Just because he was a dog didn't mean Arf couldn't have dreams. To fly like a bird was all he ever wanted.

PRACTICE WITH ME
Story Beginnings

Are you having a hard time getting started? Let's practice together! We'll use my story ingredients and try different ideas.

There are many ways to begin a story. Can you guess the most famous way? That's right: *Once upon a time.* You can always start that way if you are stuck. If I were to use that beginning, my story would start: *Once upon a time there was a polar bear.*

Remember that your readers haven't met your character yet. So you can begin your story by introducing your character. Pick out one or two things that make your character very interesting. I might say something like: *Once there was a purple polar bear named Pete. He loved pineapples!*

Who ever heard of a purple, pineapple-popping Polar Bear?

SHIP TO:
Pete the
Polar
Bear

It is a great idea to put a problem into the beginning. Starting with a problem makes the reader pay attention. Here's how my story might start with a problem: *Pete the polar bear didn't have any friends. The Arctic animals laughed at him because he was purple. They made fun of him because he hated the cold!* That was really more than one problem, wasn't it? But remember, having lots of problems is good for a story.

You can also start your story with action. Readers really love action! Here's my story with some action to kick it off: *Wham! Another snowball hit Pete in the head. Why didn't any of the other animals like him? he wondered.*

HERE'S A TIP

For a good start to your story, introduce your character and introduce a problem.

Extra Food for Thought

If you are hungry for more, there is another ingredient for you to think about. It is called **dialogue.** It is pronounced "die-a-log." Dialogue is when the characters talk.

You can use dialogue anywhere in your story. But you can also start your story with dialogue. Here is an example:

"I can't take it!" Pete the polar bear said. "It's too cold here at the North Pole."

Did you notice the **quotation marks**? They look kind of like two floating commas. They are used to show that a character is talking.

Dialogue is fun. But the rules about writing dialogue are hard. If you haven't learned the rules yet, that's okay. Go ahead and make your characters talk anyway if you want to.

Chapter 7

Turn Up the Heat

In a recipe, the directions take you step-by-step. There is an order you follow. The **plot** of a story is like that. It is the order that things happen in your story. The plot is made up of the action and the conflict.

A plot has a beginning, a middle, and an ending. You already have a good beginning for your story. So the middle comes next. This is where the problems in your story really heat up!

WRITING YOUR STORY'S MIDDLE

The middle of the story might take you a long time. But it is a very fun part to write. Your character will try to fix the problems. But don't let him fix them all right away. Your character might have to try again and again before he fixes them. Or maybe the character fixes the first problem, but then a new problem turns up!

Just remember: Leave at least one big problem to be fixed at the end.

You can also add more of other ingredients to the middle. They will make your story longer and more interesting. Maybe your main character has a family or friends. They could become extra characters in your story. Maybe your character has an enemy! An enemy would probably cause new problems. You can also have more than one setting in your story. Each setting gives you the chance to add lots of descriptive details. In my story, Pete travels from the Arctic to Hawaii.

Some writers figure out their plot as they write. If you are ready to write the middle of your story, then get going! Other writers like to make a plan before they write. If that sounds like you, keep reading.

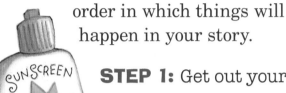

PRACTICE WITH ME
Make a Plot Outline

Do you want to plan the middle of your story before you write it? There is a tool that can help. It is called a plot **outline**. An outline lists the order in which things will happen in your story.

STEP 1: Get out your list of story problems. Which ones would make your story the most interesting? If you think of new problems, add them to the list. It's not too late!

STEP 2: Did you use a problem in your story beginning? Mark that Problem #1. Does it seem like one of the other problems should come next? Mark that Problem #2.

STEP 3: Keep numbering the other problems that you want to use. You might use two or three, or maybe many more!

STEP 4: Make a new copy of your problem list. This time, list the problems in the right order. Leave out any problems you don't plan to use. Now you have your outline.

I followed these same steps to make my outline. Here is what it looks like:

★ Problem #1: My polar bear can't handle being cold.

★ Problem #2: My polar bear feels lonely because he doesn't have many friends.

★ Problem #3: My polar bear gets laughed at because he is purple.

★ Problem #4: My polar bear decides to go to Hawaii. But how can he get there?

★ Problem #5: My polar bear makes an ice raft, but it melts!

★ Problem #6: My polar bear gets lost.

★ Problem #7: My polar bear needs water skis. But they don't make water skis for polar bears!

When you have finished your own outline, you might want to review pages 26–27. Then use your outline as a guide to help you write the middle of your story. Add details to make your middle interesting. Your story will grow and grow!

HERE'S A TIP

Remember not to solve all the problems too early in your story. Keep the heat on!

Chapter 8 Out of the Oven

When cookies are golden brown, they are done baking. It is time to take them out of the oven. But it's a little harder to know when it is time to finish a story.

There are no rules about when a story has to end. But you can ask yourself some questions. Does your story have a great beginning? Have you used lots of ingredients in the middle of your story? Has your character tried to solve the problems in many different ways? Then maybe it is time for the ending.

So, do you just stop writing? No! How the story ends is very important. If you write an interesting ending, your readers will be satisfied. They will feel like they do when they have eaten a special treat.

So what needs to happen for readers to feel satisfied? The character needs to fix the problems that are left. That is why the reader kept reading. Now is your chance for the big moment of the story. It is called the **resolution.** The resolution comes when all the problems are finally fixed.

Brainstorming Activity

Write an Ending

STEP 1: Read over your story. Start at the beginning and go all the way through. Have you included a lot of action and details? Has there been a lot of conflict? Are there more things you want to add to the middle? Or does it seem like it is time for the story to end?

STEP 2: What problems did you leave to be fixed at the end? Try some brainstorming. You are very good at it by now! What ideas do you have for how to fix these final problems? Make a list. Use your imagination! Is there some way to give your reader a surprise? That can be a fun way to end your story.

STEP 3: Read over your ideas. Which ending would be the most exciting? Which one would make the reader feel the most satisfied? Pick the one you like best.

STEP 4: Think about how the character will feel when the problems are all gone. He or she will feel different than they did at the beginning. Will your character be happy at the end? Proud? Tired? Excited? All of those things? Put these feelings in your ending.

PRACTICE WITH ME
The Ending

Are you having trouble with your ending? I bet my polar bear story can help. You can read it now if you want. The whole story is on pages 41–45. Study how Pete fixes the problems he has in the story. Do all his problems seem to be fixed at the end? How did Pete's feelings change from the beginning to the ending?

After thinking about my story, write an ending for your story.

HERE'S A TIP

Sometimes it is hard to end a story because you like your character so much. But you don't have to say good-bye. Write the ending to this story now. Later you can start a new adventure using the same character!

Chapter 9 Tempting Titles

Now your story has a beginning, a middle, and an ending. It is packed full of ingredients. But your story still doesn't have a name. The name of a story is called the **title.**

Maybe you already have some ideas for your title. Remember that readers will look at the title first. The title should tempt the readers, or make them hungry to get to the story.

Brainstorming Activity

Add a Title

STEP 1: Read through your whole story again. Write down the titles that come into your head. Remember to write down all your ideas, even the silly ones.

STEP 2: Think about the kind of story you have written. The title can tell the reader what kind of story it is. If you have written a mystery, you can use that in the title: *The Mystery of the Purple Polar Bear.* If you have written an adventure story, let your reader know: *The Adventures of Pete the Polar Bear.* Add more title ideas to your brainstorming list.

STEP 3: Look at your characters, setting, and problems. Look at all your story ingredients. Which ones do you think are the most interesting? Use those ingredients to think of more new titles. For example, my title, *Silly, Chilly Bear,* tells something about the kind of story I wrote, the setting, and my character.

STEP 4: Look at all of the title ideas on your list. Which one will make a reader want to gobble up your story? Pick the one you like the best. Write it at the top of your story. Underneath, write "A story by" and then add your name. That is how writers tell the world it is their story!

HERE'S A TIP

Pick a title that will grab your readers' attention!

Chapter 10
Taste Test

You have written all the way to the end of your story. But you aren't done yet! It is time for a taste test. Remember, this was just your rough draft. If you were making cookies, you would probably eat one now. But what if it didn't taste right? You might need to add more ingredients before you bake the next batch. Or, you might need to bake the cookies a little longer.

A rough draft is like that, too. Reading it tells you what else your story needs to make it taste just right. Do you need to work on it a little longer? You might decide to add some new ingredients. You might want to take something out. This is your chance to **revise** your story. That means making changes. You want to make it the best story possible.

REVISE YOUR STORY

STEP 1: How can you make your story better? Here are some things to ask yourself. Think about them while you read through your rough draft.

★ Does the reader know a lot about my characters?

★ Did I use my five senses to create details?

★ Does my story have plenty of action?

★ Do the problems grab the reader's attention right away?

★ Does the main character continue to have problems throughout the story?

★ Are all of the problems fixed when the story is done?

STEP 2: When you are done reading, it is time to revise. You might want to find an eraser now! You will also see why it is a good idea to double-space. It leaves you lots of room to make changes and add new things.

Go through your whole story again. But this time, revise the things you want to change. Use the blank lines to add new words or sentences.

Cross things out that you don't like. Use arrows to show where you want to move things. Erase a word to change it to a better word.

STEP 3: You might need to go through your rough draft more than once. Don't stop until your story is great!

STEP 4: After revising, your sloppy copy will be *extra* sloppy! If it is too hard to read, you'll need to copy the story onto a clean sheet of paper. That will make it easier for you to do our next activity.

ARF THE FLYING DOG RUFF!

I Once ~~there was~~ had a dog named ARF. He never ~~liked to~~ play with other dogs? or play fetch. He would spend all day watching the birds in his yard. How come they can fly and I can't? Where do they go when they fly away? I want to ~~fly away~~ like the birds too. Arf practiced jumping into always fell to the

Add the BIG CITY to the part about the day they're here.

HERE'S A TIP

Revising is very important. Don't skip this step! Revise until your story is as good as you can make it!

Chapter 11
Borrow Some Sugar

Earlier I told you not to worry too much about the rules of writing. Maybe you just guessed how to spell something. Well, now the time has come to fix those things! When you have finished revising your story, it is time to **edit.** That means to fix the things that are wrong. This is the step where the rules matter.

Grab that eraser. Go back over your story very carefully. Look up words you don't know. Fix your mistakes. You might also notice more things you want to revise in your story. That is okay too. Revising and editing sometimes go together.

Your eraser is a good editing tool. But there is something else that can be helpful. That is an **editor!** An editor is a person who helps you make your story better. When you cook, sometimes you need to borrow an ingredient from a neighbor. When you write, sometimes you need to borrow some editing help. I needed an editor's help to finish this book.

Your editor can help with things like spelling. Your editor can also give you other ideas for your story.

Who do you know that might edit your story for you? Is there someone in your family who could help? A teacher? A neighbor? A babysitter?

Maybe you want to ask a friend to be your editing partner. Both of you can write your own stories. Then, you can trade and edit each other's stories.

Tell your editors what kind of help you need. Here are the kinds of questions to ask:

★ Is there anyplace where the story doesn't make sense?

★ Does the story have enough action and conflict?

★ Did you want to keep reading?

★ Do you know enough about the characters?

★ Was the ending satisfying?

★ Did I make any spelling or writing mistakes?

★ What did you like best about my story?

Pay attention to your editors. Sometimes their ideas will be really great! But it is your story. You do not have to change it if you don't want to.

HERE'S A TIP

Don't forget to ask your editors what they like about your story. Ask them for some "sugar." Ask them to say something nice. It is fun to hear good things after you have worked so hard!

Chapter 12

Share the Feast

Writers need readers just like cooks need eaters. Now that you have created a great story, it is time to share it!

You can share your story with your family. You can share your story with your friends and neighbors. Ask your teacher, too. Maybe you can share your story for show-and-tell at school.

SHARE YOUR STORY

There are many different ways you can share your story. Here are just a few ideas:

Turn your story into a book. Use new pieces of paper. Write a fresh copy of your story. Do you want to add pictures? If you do, remember to leave space for them. Make a cover out of colored paper. Staple the pages inside the cover.

Type your story into the computer. Are you learning how to type on a computer? Use your story for practice. When you are done typing, you can print it out. Maybe someone can help you email it to your friends and family.

Read your story out loud.
Practice reading your story out loud.
Then invite your friends and family
to hear you read it. You can even
serve popcorn like they do at the
movies!

Make a recording of your story.
If you have a tape recorder, tape
yourself reading your story. You can
send the tape to friends who are
far away.

**Turn your story into puppet
theater.** Act out your story using
puppets or stuffed animals. Ask a
friend to help you. Or your friend
can watch while you tell the story.

Maybe you have some puppets in
your toy box. Or you can make
puppets out of paper lunch bags or
old socks.

Go online. Want to see your
story in print or on the Web? One
magazine that publishes young
people's stories is *Stone Soup*. Visit
their web site, www.stonesoup.com,
for information on how to submit a
story. You'll also find links to other
magazines, online story sites, and
writing contests.

What other ways can you think
of to share your story?

Chapter 13
Are You Still Hungry?

Congratulations! If you have followed the story-writing recipe in this book, then you are a story writer. Good for you!

Now that you have had a taste of story-writing, I bet you want some more! The good news is that you can write as many stories as you want. Just go back to the beginning of this book. Then follow the recipe all over again. To get a different story, you just need to change your ingredients. It will be like making chocolate chip instead of sugar cookies.

This time, pick a different animal or a person for your character. Choose a different place for your setting. Pick a different activity. Go through each story step with your new ingredients. You will write a whole new story.

Or you can try a whole different *kind* of story. Writers get ideas for stories from all around them. Write about the things you like. Just remember to include all the ingredients you have learned about. Here are some ideas to get you started:

★ Write a story about a holiday.

★ Write a story using your family and friends as characters.

★ Write a story about the funniest thing you can think of.

★ Write a story about one of your toys coming alive.

★ Fill in the blank: I wish I had a story about _____ .

HERE'S A TIP

One of the most important ingredients you can add to your story is— FUN!

SILLY, CHILLY BEAR

A story by Lisa Bullard

Here is the story I wrote using the story-writing recipe. You may remember some of it from our writing practices. Now you can read the whole thing. You can even edit it if you want some editing practice.

"I can't take it anymore!" Pete the polar bear cried. He was shivering hard. "It's too cold. There's nothing here but ice and snow. I want to go someplace warm. Maybe then I could stop shivering long enough to make friends."

"You're such a baby!" said Artie the Arctic fox. "You're the only polar bear who gets cold. I bet it's because you are purple!"

Pete growled through his sharp teeth. Artie darted away.

"I'm your friend, Pete," said Nick the narwhal. "I asked some of the other whales about your problem. They told me you should move to a place called Hawaii."

"What's it like there?" asked Pete.

"Well, I hear Hawaii has warm winds that smell like flowers. Farmers there grow lots of sweet, juicy pineapples. Friendly people and bright colors are everywhere."

"Dude!" said Pete. "That sounds like the home for me. How can I get there?"

Pete and Nick thought hard. Suddenly Pete said, "I have it! You can cut me an ice raft using your long tusk. I'll float to Hawaii!"

Pete settled onto the very edge of the ice, right where it met the sea.

Crack! Crack! Nick's tusk cut through the ice around Pete. Soon Pete was sitting in the middle of an ice raft. Nick pushed him out to sea. Pete was on his way!

Every morning Pete took his bath. Every morning the water felt a little warmer. Pete was so happy he didn't notice that the ice raft was melting! The raft shrank more each day. One morning, Pete woke up to find his feet in the water. The raft was barely big enough to hold him!

Pete jumped up. What was he going to do? Soon he would sink into the ocean.

Suddenly Pete noticed a tiny speck far, far away. Maybe that is Hawaii, Pete thought. Polar bears are good swimmers. I'll just have to swim.

So Pete swam and swam. The speck got bigger and bigger. It was an island! There were palm trees and a white, sandy beach. Pete raced to shore. My new home, he thought and smiled.

But the more Pete looked around, the more his smile turned to a frown. There were no friendly people. There weren't even any pineapples! He was the only one there.

Pete buried his head in his big front paws. At least back home he'd had Nick. Here he had nobody.

Suddenly a deep voice said, "What's the matter, Pete?"

Pete looked out to sea. A huge humpback whale was looking back at him.

"Do I know you?" asked Pete.

"My name's Henry," said the whale. "I'm Nick's cousin. He told the family about you. He said to watch for a purple polar bear."

"I sure am glad to see you. I'm stuck here all alone." Pete sighed. Then he smacked his paw against his forehead.

"Wait a minute!" he said. "I've got a great idea! Are you willing to help me, Henry?"

"Sure," said Henry, "Any friend of Nick's is a friend of mine."

So Pete used his sharp teeth to cut down a palm tree. He twisted the leaves together to make a long, thick rope. He used his sharp claws to scrape the trunk into a long, flat board. He used the white sand to rub the board smooth.

He asked Henry if he could tie the rope around Henry's tail. Henry agreed. Pete put the board in the water. He stood on the board and held onto the other end of the rope.

"Ready, set, go!" he shouted. Henry moved his powerful body through the water, pulling Pete behind. "Hawaii, here I come!" yelled Pete.

Pete was water-skiing his way to Hawaii! Soon he saw another island ahead of them. But this island was different. Pete could see hundreds of people on the sandy beach. He could see surfers riding the waves. He saw red, orange, yellow, green, and blue everywhere. He could even smell flowers!

"Hold up, Henry," he called. Henry stopped. "Thanks, friend," said Pete, untying the rope from around Henry's tail. "I can take it from here. Say hi to Nick for me. And come visit sometime!"

"You bet, friend," said Henry, "Surf's up, Dude!"

"Surf's up!" said Pete. He rode the next big wave all the way onto the beach.

"Pineapple smoothies for everyone—my treat!" said Pete. All the people cheered. Pete lay down and kissed the warm sand. He grinned. This is the perfect home for a purple polar bear, he thought.

Glossary

brainstorming: thinking up many different ideas

character: an animal, person, or creature in a story

conflict: problems in a story

descriptive details: information that describes, or tells more about, something

dialogue: the words that characters say in a story

edit: to fix the mistakes in a story

editor: a person who helps fix the mistakes and make a story better

emotions: the feelings a character has, such as happiness, anger, or fear

fantasy: a story that includes things that don't exist in the real world, such as make-believe places or talking animals

fiction: a story that is made up

five senses: seeing, hearing, touching, smelling, and tasting

flavorings: things added to food to make it taste a certain way

ingredients: different things that are mixed together to make something else

interview: a conversation in which you ask somebody lots of questions

outline: a written plan that tells the order in which things will happen in a story

plot: the action and conflict that happen from the beginning, to the middle, to the end of a story

quotation marks: punctuation that goes around the outside of dialogue

realistic: like real life. A realistic story is one that includes lots of facts or other details of the actual world.

recipe: step-by-step directions that tell you how to cook something

resolution: the point at the end of the story when all the problems are fixed

revise: to make changes in a story to make it better

rough draft: a sloppy copy

setting: the place and the time of a story

title: the name of a story

For Further Reading

Arthur Writes a Story
by Marc Brown
Little, Brown, 1996

From Pictures to Words:
A Book About Making
a Book
by Janet Stevens
Holiday House, 1995

If You Were a Writer
by Joan Lowery Nixon
Aladdin, 1995

Look at My Book:
How Kids Can
Write & Illustrate
Terrific Books
by Loreen Leedy
Holiday House, 2004

Nothing Ever
Happens on
90th Street
by Roni Schotter
Scholastic, 1999

What Do Authors Do?
by Eileen Christelow
Clarion Books, 1997

You Have to Write
by Janet S. Wong
Margaret K. McElderry,
2002

Index

action, 7, 25, 26
brainstorming, 5;
   problems in your story, 18
   setting details, 14
   titles, 33
characters, 7, 10–13, 21;
   in story beginnings,
     24, 25
   in story endings, 31
   in story middles, 26–27
conflict, 18, 26. *See also*
   problems

descriptive details:
   about characters, 12
   about settings, 14,
     16, 27
dialogue, 25
editing, 36–37
emotions, 21, 31
fiction, 8
outlining the plot, 28–29
parts of a story:
   beginnings, 22–25
   endings, 30–31
   middles, 26–29

plot, 26, 27, 28–29
problems: 18–21;
   in story beginnings, 25
   in story endings, 30–31
   in story middles, 26–28
quotation marks, 25
resolution, 30
revising, 34–35, 36

LISA BULLARD started writing stories as soon as she knew how to create words. Now that she's a grown-up, she's fortunate enough to be living her childhood dream as the author of several children's books. They include the picture books *Not Enough Beds!* and the award-winning *Trick-or-Treat on Milton Street.*

As a visiting author and part of the COMPAS "Writers & Artists in the Schools" program, Lisa has taught thousands of students about story-writing. All of the activities in *You Can Write a Story* have been improved with the help of those enthusiastic young writers.

Lisa lives in Minneapolis, Minnesota, with two cats (one has a tail and one doesn't), lots of books, snow globes from around the world, and extra beds for her visiting nephews and nieces.

School visits give Lisa new ideas all the time, so check out her web site at www.lisabullard.com. There you will find activities and links for even more writing fun!

DEBORAH HALEY MELMON first realized she would be an artist when a papier-mâché lion she created in her seventh-grade art class grew so large that it had to be driven home in the trunk of her parent's Oldsmobile with the lid up! Since her graduation from Academy of Art College, in San Francisco, California, she has illustrated games, books and playful educational materials for children, including life-size murals for Discovery Rooms at the California Science Center in Los Angeles and advertisements for Legoland San Diego.

Deborah lives in Menlo Park, California, with two energetic Airedale terriers. She divides her time between her studio, her dogs and the golf course. You can see more of her work on her website at www.debmelmonstudio.com.